BRIDGES TO HOPE

ALVIN N. ROGNESS

AUGSBURG PUBLISHING HOUSE
Minneapolis, Minnesota

CONTENTS

About Bridges and Hope

The key to each chapter in this book is the refrain of the psalmist, "In thee, O Lord, do I hope."

Since the whole of life is the Lord's, he may use many means (or bridges) to bring us the gift. If we let him be "in, with, and under" the events or experiences of life, it is possible that even times of adversity, failure, or grief may each become a strange bridge spanning the gulf from meaninglessness to hope.

While our hope is *in* the Lord, our hope is also *for* something. And this something is in the future, something yet to be. If we are counting on the Lord, we will need to hope for that which is pleasing to *him*. This may radically modify the catalog of our hopes. That which initially we had hoped for may turn out to be something we would not want at all.

It is my prayer that each of the subjects in this book may, under God, lead us to hope.

1

Hope: Gift
or Achievement?

Hope is one of the gifts the Lord is eager to give. Hope is also a state of mind we are anxious to achieve.

If someone is at your door with a package, a gift, there are several things you must *do* before the gift really is yours. You must hear the doorbell, you must open the door, and you must let the package be put in your hands. After it is in your hands, it is of course still a gift.

Since every good thing in life is a gift from God, and since hope is a good thing, it will inevitably be something for which we thank God. If, on the other hand we do nothing but sit quietly in a chair and wait for the gift to overcome us, there would be no point in my writing this book or in your reading it.

God may use a variety of means to convey the gift: events, experiences, people, knowledge, beliefs. These we call *bridges*. We cross them to reach hope. In a profounder sense it is God who crosses them, or uses them, to give us hope. All good gifts are from him, including hope. We need only to be vigilant not to hinder God from bringing the gift.

Any assurance that he is currently around, and that he comes bearing gifts, must have its roots in the one towering event of his coming. He came in Jesus Christ centuries ago. Christ lived and died and rose again. We believe that he came because he loved us, and we believe that in some strange and wonderful way he opened the way again for man to come to God, and for God to come to man. All the riches of the kingdom of God are now available to us, including hope.

The word *hope* may be used in more than one way, and will be throughout this book. When we say, "Hope in the Lord," we are really saying that we count on God, we rely on him, we rest back in his arms, we trust him. When, on the other hand, we say, "Don't lose hope," we most likely are referring to something we are anxious to have, or to have happen, in the future.

If we seem to say that future looks hopeless, we may only be saying that the kind of civilization we have known in these last hundred years is not likely to continue. And very likely we conclude that such an outcome would not be good. Generally speaking, we like this style of life, with two cars for each family, a college education for everyone, central heating and air-conditioning, recreational opportunities for all, and unlimited variety of commodities in our stores.

I confess that I would like this for my grandchildren—a world at peace, with relative abundance for everyone. Given the wisdom and the will to follow the ways of God, I believe this should be possible for all peoples on this earth. On the other hand, there may be other styles of life that could give my grandchildren a chance to become great and good people. Only God knows.

No matter what changes may come in our styles of life, most of all I want my grandchildren to "hope in the Lord." They may have little faith that the world will remain as it has been, but they may still have courage and faith and *hope,* if they count on God to guide them and hold them.

As a boy, I lived in a village. We had no running

water, no radio or television, no automobiles, no telephone. Our food was adequate, but certainly not exotic. Looking back, I remember this as the good life. Frankly, I would not elect to return to these more primitive conditions, but I certainly cannot conclude that they were intolerable. There is no single style of life that can guarantee happiness, righteousness, or even security.

You may be as content and happy with a walk in the woods as with a Caribbean cruise, as cheerful riding a bicycle as a Cadillac, as healthy with a simple meal as a lavish one, as charitable with little money as with much. The key to a fulfilled life is not in the abundance of things; the key is in hope.

It is not strange that hope is hard to come by in our day. This century has seen volcanic changes. Two massive wars and several smaller ones have shaken the earth. Technology has escalated with one surprise after another, giving us unheard-of powers and options. Television and radio have plummeted the world's problems into our living rooms. Voices, many of them pessimistic, warn us that unprecedented adjustments are before us. It is not strange that we tremble a bit. We are much more comfortable with things as they have been. We naturally fear the unknown.

By the same token, hope becomes a prize ardently to be desired and pursued. We do not want to lose our footing. We want some solid place to stand, if storms of change are swirling about us.

And there is a place to stand. God is here. He has always been here. Nor is he here simply as an observer, sitting comfortably in some heavenly bleachers, watching us struggle. He is in the thick of things. He gives us freedom to blunder and to sin. But he sets limits. And he picks up the broken pieces of our failures, if we but let him.

He has a grand design for his children. He created all people to be his family. He invaded the earth in Jesus Christ (God the Son); he established an eternal kingdom in our midst; he is ceaselessly at work through the Spirit (God the Holy Ghost) to recall us to his kingdom; and he is present to guard and keep us from all evil and harm. God does not want to lose a single one of us. He wants us for the riches of his kingdom here and now, and he wants us with him in heaven forever.

The earth itself is a part of his great empire. He has placed all sorts of resources for utility and beauty on this planet for the enjoyment of his children. Earth is not a desert drear, to which he exiles us for a gloomy, probationary period.

With our hopes firmly resting in him we have a right to unpredictable hope for a future on the earth. He gives the gift, and we are to exhaust its rich possibilities.

Scripture: Isaiah 40:18-31

Dear God, you created us for this earth in love, and you redeemed us to give us a kingdom to inhabit while here. Within the kingdom you are lavish with gifts, including hope. Help us, by the Holy Spirit, to accept this gift of hope and to live in it. Amen.

2

Is Fear Bad?

When Jesus repeatedly warned against fear ("Fear not, O you of little faith"), he was talking about excessive worry and anxiety over things that might happen sometime in the future. This kind of fear is bad. It saps our strength for today's tasks. Each of us is like a ship, designed to carry a cargo that belongs to today. If we insist on loading the ship also with tomorrow's cargo, the craft will flounder.

But there are fears that we ought to have. If you see a tornado coming, it would be foolhardy not to be afraid and not to take precautions to get out of its way. If a tiger is crouching above you in a tree ready to leap, any bravado you might display would hardly be called courage. You ought to be afraid.

Years ago, during a national depression, when people were in panic, President Roosevelt, in allaying the people's fears, coined a phrase, "The only thing we have to fear is fear itself." It was a good phrase, and people needed to hear it. But it certainly is not altogether true. If the flood waters are rising and your home is in the path of the overflowing river, it isn't enough simply to fear the fear that threatens you. You fear the threatening waters.

Lewis Browne opens his book *This Believing World* with the sentence, "In the beginning was fear, and fear was in the hearts of men, and fear controlled men." It is as natural to have fear as life itself. One after another of the forces in nature which created fear in primitive man have been understood and harnessed. But there is still the vast unknown, the very mystery of existence, that generates uneasiness and fear in man. We would be less than human if this were not so.

There is yet another kind of fear—which is good. In his explanations of the ten commandments, Luther prefaces each paragraph with the words, "We should fear and love God. . . ." If God is our great and good Father, and we the children whom he loves, why should we fear him? It is a good question.

In fact, we should fear him in two ways.

First, we should fear his judgment, his wrath. This is true even for the Christian who lives in the promise, "There is therefore now no condemnation for those who are in Christ Jesus." After all, as a Christian I am still a kind of dual person. I am the old Adam, and I am the new man in Christ. I am a Dr. Jekyll and Mr. Hyde. I am a bad man, and I am a good man. The bad man in me needs constantly to stand before the judgment of God in terror. Luther talks about the bad man in the Christian needing daily to be drowned. He needs to be brought to his knees in a cry for mercy.

It would be a pity if we never got beyond this kind of fear. It is the fear of the slave for his tyrant master, the fear of the criminal for his executioner, the fear of the sinner standing convicted in the high court. It is the profound fear of one who lives in the universe without hope, the fear of one who sees no hope either in this life or in the world to come.

God wants us to have this kind of fear. To create it is the deep purposes of his law. He wants us driven to the wall, to collapse, to have nowhere to turn. It is the necessary preface, or prelude, to the surprisingly good news that he has in store for us. Without this fear, we would never revel in the good news.

The good news is that he, God himself, has taken our guilt and judgment upon himself. The judge steps down from his bench to take our place in the dock, and to go to his death for us. This is the strange turn in the courtroom of God. Suddenly everything is changed. We are now the innocent and he the guilty. We are conveyed from the courtroom to the foot of the cross. We are beyond the reach of judgment. We are free in Christ. Fear of judgment is replaced by the wonder of his mercy. And all this by grace alone through faith.

But a new kind of fear emerges, the fear of the child that he might displease his father. And this is a good fear. This is altogether different from the courtroom fear. This is not a fear that if we fail to please him, he will evict us from the home and no longer be our father. This is not a fear that if we do not obey his commandments, we can no longer be his child. We are his, by grace, through Christ, come what may. This is the fear born out of profound gratitude, gratitude for being claimed by him "without any merit or worthiness in me."

God is pleased with this kind of fear, for it is the work of the Holy Spirit in the believer. It is evidence that his child is caught up in the wonder of God's incredible love, and now is in earnest about wanting to please him and thank him.

But let us come back to the kind of crippling fear that God wants to drive out—the fear that is bad.

When I lie sleepless at night with worries and anxieties and fears, in almost every instance I am carrying tomorrow's cargo. Something bad may happen to me tomorrow. I don't know what it may be. I may get cancer, I may die, I may lose my job, my children may get into trouble.

13

Like a swarm of gnats these fears torment me, and I can't sleep.

At that point, God in effect says, "Go to sleep. Everything will be all right." Everything may not be all right, of course. You may get cancer. Your children may get into trouble. But whatever happens, God will see you through. Besides, many of your fears are totally groundless. Most of these things will not happen, and you are wasting precious nervous energy.

Remember those beautiful passages in Matthew 6 in which Jesus speaks of the birds of the air, the lilies and grasses of the field, and says, "Are you not much better than they? Your heavenly Father knows that you have need."

If we are to come to terms with the various kinds of fears, we will need to rest back in the wonder of God's love and daily care. Only then can we be released for love and for hope.

All the tomorrows will be overcast with the dark clouds of the unknown, and hope will die, until we package our fears and leave them with this great and loving heavenly Father. And this is precisely what he likes to have us do.

Scripture: Matthew 6:24-34

How wonderful, O Lord, that we may put it all in your hands—our sins, our fears, our tomorrows. Give us the ability to do just that, so that we may face every day with love for you and for our neighbors and with courage and hope whatever may come. Amen.

3

Can We Know God's Plans?

When God created man, he planned that man should live in unbroken joy and fellowship with him forever.

When God sent his Son, Jesus Christ, to the earth, he planned to recover man from the bondage of sin and Satan and to reinstate him with full rights to the kingdom forever.

When the Holy Spirit was given, God made clear his intention to summon and reshape man into his image again, and to usher him at death into the fulness of the kingdom.

We need have no doubts about these three sweeping purposes of God. Whatever serves to achieve these ends for each of us, and for the world, will obviously be within the will of God.

It is also safe to conclude that God wants everything good for us these swift years on the earth. He has "put all things under his feet" in this universe for man to use, to care for, and to enjoy. The earth is not a kind of concentration camp, where we are on probation for three score years and ten before being promoted to heaven. The earth is the Lord's, and its fabulous riches are here for enjoyment. He wants these years to be rich and full for his children whom he loves.

In any given instance, God alone knows what precisely

may be good for us. He has cautioned us that "my thoughts are not your thoughts, neither are your ways my ways." What I desire for myself may not be what God desires at all.

I may want wealth or power or fame. God, in his greater wisdom, may know that the achieving of these ends would only make it more difficult for him to remake me into the kind of person he wants me to be, so he may actually keep me from becoming rich, or from being elected to office, or from having people fawn over me. If he doesn't actually stand in the way, he may give me little help.

My hopes for myself, or for my world, will always need to be tentative. They are legitimate only if they coincide with God's hopes for me. Does God want me to be rich? Only if riches will not control me and destroy me. Does God want me to have power? Only if I use this power for the good of myself and others. He may know that I am the kind of person whom power would damage and ruin, and in his wise providence he may prevent me from wielding power.

I may thwart God's will. I am not a puppet. He has given me the gift of freedom, the right of independence. His fears for me notwithstanding, I may elbow my way to wealth and power. At that point he will of course use every resource to see that I use these things for good, but he may fail. Wealth and power may plunge me into ruin.

God would be an unloving God if he did not checkmate many of my hopes. If a five-year-old boy had his heart set on having a bicycle and a gun, his father would be both stupid and cruel to have these dangerous tools placed in his hands. Our heavenly father is no less loving. He will guard us against some of our fondest hopes.

I like the kind of civilization that has emerged. I like

football games, the convenience of automobiles, airplanes, computers, electricity, central heating. What stake does God have in this kind of civilization? I think he wants these gifts to be mine. Otherwise, why would he have put these resources in his universe? Why would he have given us the probing minds to ferret out these things? But if he should find it easier to reshape me into the kind of person that resembles him by having me ride the back of a donkey instead of in a jetliner, then he probably has no stake at all in keeping this sort of civilization going.

I think he wants me to have a minimum of tragedy, pain, and sorrow. But, if by being spared these disasters, I become a proud and self-righteous prig, he would have no interest in sparing me those hardships and adversities. He might actually design some disappointments, so that I might grow in humility, generosity, mercy, and understanding.

Looking back on our lives, most of us can attribute something good coming out of adversity. We had hopes, but they were shattered. For a time, we wondered if God cared at all. By some strange turn, we began to see that God was working something rather wonderful out of the shattered pieces, much like a little girl with a broken doll discovering that a brand new doll is hers to replace the old one.

One thing is certain: God wants for us only that which is good. If his good plans for us are lost, either through our own stupidity or selfishness or that of others, he has other good plans to replace the ones that are lost. He can always pick up the pieces or provide something new.

It is difficult to imagine that God does not want us to enjoy the magnificent dividends of modern technology. Think of the drudgery that the machine has eliminated. Would he not want this for the whole world? Is it not

17

right for me to entertain hopes that my grandchildren will enjoy the kind of "abundant" life science has made possible? And in addition, that they may know a world in which war and injustice may in large measure be overcome? The very power which technology has put into our hands, properly managed, can usher in a whole, new, and wonderful era in the history of the world.

And should it be more difficult for God to reshape his children into the creatures of love and mercy which belong to his kingdom if they work a 40-hour week, or even a 30-hour week, than if they work 10 hours a day and 6 or 7 days a week? And should I be less eligible for the kingdom if I ride a tractor than if I drive oxen?

To be sure, my hopes for well-being must expand to include all people everywhere. It will not do to limit myself to my family or my country. And when I include the whole world, I may have to discipline myself to sacrifices which may not always be pleasant. We of the "have" nations may have to scale down our expectations and hopes to include the rights and the hopes of the "have-not" nations. All are God's children, after all, and God's plans for them may condition his plans for us.

God has great plans for his children the world over, here and hereafter forever. He has given us freedom, the awesome power to disobey him and to detour his plans. But he does not give up. He forgives and restores. He has great hopes for us.

Scripture: Isaiah 55

When our fondest hopes fail, help us to remember that you are not at the end of your rope, O God. These hopes may not have been the best, and you may have better ones. Forgive us for entertaining feeble or unworthy plans, and help us to rest back in the over-all, grand plan you have for all your children. Amen.

18

4

Does Jesus Solve All Problems?

If we let Jesus take over, great things do happen. Again and again, people have testified that "when Jesus came into my heart," or "when I said yes to Jesus, my life really changed."

But does Jesus eliminate our problems? Could it be that he actually adds a few?

When he returns in glory, he will indeed eliminate them—tragedy, sorrow, pain, even death. Until then, we will continue to live in the midst of a vast network of unsolved problems.

But he does rid us of some central problems. Guilt, for instance. His life, death, and resurrection in some strange and wonderful way clears away the wreckage of sin. We are forgiven. No longer need we drag along the cargo of the past. He gives us day by day the right to a new start. He even gives us the right and the duty to forget the failures of the past. This may seem like a cop-out, but it is actually a clearing away of the debris so that we have a chance to build anew.

And Jesus deals hopelessness a hard blow. He ushers us into a kingdom that will never go under. The storms may lash away at your frail craft, toss it about, and all but capsize it, but it won't sink. You will not be lost, because Jesus is there and he holds you fast. You will live with fear, but fear will not paralyze you.

He also bends these self-centered hearts of ours. We begin to be stirred by the needs of others. This preoccupation with my neighbor's wants has an amazing way of diminishing my anxiety and fears.

Jesus does perform a major miracle when he comes. The inner orientation of my life is vastly different. In the words of Hebrews 12:1, I "lay aside every weight and sin" and I free myself for running the race. The race is still a hard one. I may slip and fall. But he is there to pick me up again, and I press on to finish with a victory that he gives me.

Granted that Jesus makes a great difference in my life, does he really make any difference in the life of the world? Are there fewer problems in the twentieth century than in the first?

The answer to this question is not easy. The forces of evil are perhaps every bit as vigorous today as then. With populations multiplied a thousand times over, life on the earth is far more complex. Who is to say that the ills of the first century have been overcome? Or, if they have, that new ones have not replaced them?

One thing is quite clear: the Bible does not promise that year by year and century by century things will be getting better and better. The forces of good and the forces of evil will be pitted against each other until the end. God and Satan are at war. To be sure, the outcome is not in question. God will win. In fact, Jesus dealt a death blow to Satan.

Any reflective reading of history, however, will show a striking advance in the basic values of life. Jesus has solved many problems. His kingdom is a leaven, working steadily and quietly to change things. When people are captured by him, they become agents to bring the standards and the values of the eternal kingdom to bear on the affairs of the earth. One after another of the cruel practices of men have been replaced by models of life reflecting justice and mercy: the rights of children and women, for instance, the institution of slavery, the care of prisoners. Even freedom in governments has come in the wake of man being regarded as a child of God. The Declaration on Human Rights adopted by the United Nations could never have been either written or adopted in the first century.

It might be easier for me, individually, if I were to bypass this Jesus and not become mixed up with him. After all, while he solves some of my problems, he gets me involved with his. And his problems are colossal. He wants to win the world. He is in the thick of the battles for justice and mercy for everyone. He pits himself against evil on a thousand fronts. Instead of sitting around with a few private problems that remain unsolved, by letting him in I take on—with him—the problems of the whole world.

Of course, these so-called private problems of mine are not small ones—for me. To be without Jesus is to be without a center for my life. Moreover, without him, I have no place to deposit my sin and guilt. I have no one but myself to rely on when fears and anxieties multiply. I am forced to close my eyes to the future. In fact, without him I become a drifter in the universe.

With him, even when it means taking on his problems as my own, I am firmly anchored in the love of God. Nothing can separate me from him or from that love. And in that love, I am a *somebody*. I have identity. I know who I am and why. I am on earth to join him in the enterprises of his kingdom.

Nor need the future look bleak. I take courage in the long record of his influence on history. I know too that, as Lord of the universe, he has resources for my future and for the future of the world that are limitless. The threat of evil in our day, more complex than the first century, is countered by the power of a God who created this complex world and who is equal to its dangers. My grandchildren may know a better world than anything we have ever known.

It would be a pity were I to elude him in order to escape being involved in the struggle, the pain, and the glory of his problems.

Far better that I plunge. Far better that I, like him, open my heart to the hurts and the struggles. Far better that I be caught up in the maelstrom of the kingdom, with all its excitement and risk, than that I hide myself in some cave of my own satisfactions and survival.

Our hope lies in the fact that people can be turned around by this Jesus. Twelve men were, and they changed the world. No one could have dreamed on the first Good Friday that in a relatively short time the name and power of Jesus would have swept through the entire Mediterranean world. Since then it has circled the earth. And today there is no name anywhere in the world so honored as the name of Jesus, even among nations that do not yet worship him as Lord.

The world is his, and the world is still his problem. He invites you and me to share it with him.

Scripture: Philippians 4:4-9

I still have problems, O Jesus, even if you are with me. I thank you that my sin and guilt are taken away, and that these needs no longer weigh me down. But I still have fear and worry and doubts. Help me with them. Then give me the will and courage to join you in taking on the injustice and pain of the world. Amen.

5

How the Holy Spirit Works

Can anyone really know how the holy Spirit works? Jesus himself cautioned Nicodemus against trying to know: "The wind blows wherever it wishes; you hear the sound it makes, but you do not know where it comes from or where it is going. It is the same with everyone who is born of the Spirit" (John 3:8 TEV). We cannot chart or program the Holy Spirit.

The one towering truth is that God is around. This is the central assurance of the doctrine of the Holy Spirit. God did not create us, then redeem us in Christ, and then leave us to ourselves on the planet. God, the Holy Spirit, is abroad, brooding over us, prodding us, calling us, ushering us into the kingdom and there day by day (through Word and Sacrament) transforming us. We are not left alone, and that is our hope.

The people of God have been more often misled and confused than helped when they have attempted to fix the ways of the Spirit. Whenever God works within us and within our world we face the awesome mystery of his presence.

The Scriptures do give some significant guidelines, however. We are told that we cannot come to Christ or confess him as Lord, except through the work of the Holy Spirit. Moreover, the Spirit assures us that we are children of God and can call him Father. The Spirit also guides us in our prayers. The eighth chapter of the book of Romans is rich with insights into the ways of the Spirit.

We are also told that in the church we may expect a rich variety of "gifts" of the Spirit. In 1 Corinthians 12, after a listing of such gifts, the apostle Paul asks, "They are not all apostles, or prophets, or teachers. Not all have the power to work miracles, or to heal diseases, or to speak in strange tongues, or to explain what is said" (TEV). And then he goes on to admonish, "Set your hearts, then, on the more important gifts," and bursts into a rhapsody on *love* as the supreme gift, in chapter 13. All other gifts fade into secondary importance, for God himself is love, and love is the fulfilling of the law.

Evidence that the Holy Spirit is at work among us is most clearly seen when we see "love, joy, peace, patience, kindness, goodness, faithfulness, humility, and self-control." These qualities do not separate or divide, and the Spirit is ready to give these to all the children of God.

Our day has seen a rather strong preoccupation with the work of the Holy Spirit, concentrating on "tongues" and "healing," as if these aspects of God's work were the clearest evidence that he is at work among us. A careful reading of the Scriptures would indicate that these "gifts" are as minor as they are extraordinary, and that to emphasize them may result in overlooking the gifts that are as major as they are ordinary. Love and mercy and joy and hope are gifts the Spirit is eager to give to all, tongues and healing only to a few.

If "tongues" is a language of praise (rarely capable of translation), how much more is the eloquence of our usual language a miracle of communication to God and to one another? If extraordinary healing is a gift, how much more is the vast scientific knowledge of medicine a miracle and gift from God? God must be given the glory for all, for all comes from him.

God is one. We speak of him as three persons in one, God the Father, God the Son, and God the Holy Spirit. But he is one God. We do not have a committee of three. May we not be helped in our worship of him if we think of him as one? God was in Christ, reconciling the world to himself on a cross. God, the Spirit, pours himself into us, baptizes us, dwells within us. God is one God.

I find myself praying to the one God. Sometimes I address Jesus, but more often (following Jesus' explicit instructions) I address God as Father. Rarely do I pray to the Holy Spirit. Certainly there would be no error in praying to the Spirit, but Jesus indicated that the Spirit would be a guide, leading me to the Father and to him. To be sure, we confront an insoluble mystery in the Trinity, and we need not worry our little minds about that. It is enough that God is very much around, and that he has opened a way to himself and to his kingdom for us.

To be assured of the Holy Spirit's presence and work among us is central to hope. Remember what happened that first Pentecost. A few scattered and frightened followers of Jesus were in a room praying. Suddenly there was a sound and flames, and the Holy Spirit came upon them. They were transformed. No longer cowering before the soldiers and crowds, they went on boldly to win a great part of the Mediterranean world for Jesus in one generation. They had received a strange power from outside themselves.

This is our hope, too. If we have to believe that we are on our own resources, alone to untangle our snarled moods and ways, and if we are on our own to face the gigantic issues that loom before this world, we would lose courage altogether. But we are not alone. A powerful presence is among us, working within us and around us.

I am a copilot. Everything goes pretty well, as long as the pilot is at my side. I may seem to manage the craft very well on my own. But if the pilot's seat is empty, I am victim of panic or paralysis or both. And when the navigation gets really rough, I need his hand.

We all are like that. We were never designed to go this life alone. We are profoundly dependent beings. It is in the awareness that God is at our side, within us and around us, that we become calm and bold—and competent. Knowing our own dependence is the first need; knowing his presence is the second. Paul said, "When I am weak, then am I strong." I am strong in the strength of another.

We need not know precisely how he is around or how he works. Let us leave that to the unpredictable wonder of his ways. To assume that we can manipulate or marshall the Holy Spirit to achieve ends that we have designed may be an affront to him. It is enough that we preach and teach and hear the Word with truth and fidelity and that we receive with gratitude the sacraments he has given. And to do the works of love among one another! The Holy Spirit will be there to do his amazing work within us, among us, and in our world. We do not control him; he sets out to control us.

Scripture: Romans 8:1-17
Galatians 5:16-26

Open my heart, O God, to all the gifts you are anxious to give me. Most of all, I pray for those qualities you want all your children to have. Keep me from envying or demeaning those who have different gifts from mine. Above all, give me the gift of love for you and for all. Amen.

6

The Importance of Doctrine

A doctrine is something you believe. An axiom is something you know. Two plus two equal four is an axiom. Belief in God is a doctrine.

You can demonstrate two plus two in any number of ways. Two elephants and two elephants are four elephants; put two toothpicks with two other toothpicks and you will always have four toothpicks. In no possible way can you demonstrate the existence of God in this way.

What you believe may be every bit as important as what you know, perhaps even more important. Doctrine determines life.

Hope for yourself and for the future will rest somewhat on what you know about yourself and the universe. It may rest even more on what you believe about yourself and the universe. Beliefs (doctrines) sprout wings and carry you off, in one direction or another. Let us examine what difference it may make if you believe, or do not believe, the central doctrine of our faith.

I believe in God the Father Almighty, Maker of heaven and earth.

If you really believe this, as the Bible teaches, you will conclude that you are very important in the scheme of things. You are like God, in his image. You are no biological accident. God himself has his eye on you, from the time of your birth until your death, and on into eternity.

Not only has he his eye on you; he loves you. He wants you to live with him here and hereafter forever. He watches over you. He guards and keeps you from evil and from harm. When you stumble and fall, he picks you up again.

Moreover, he honors you with management of this earth for him. He gives you freedom, he makes you responsible, and he holds you accountable. You are not a nobody, you are a somebody. You have status. You are a maker of history, not a pawn to be moved capriciously here and there by fate.

This doctrine is not altogether comfortable. As his child you have both awesome worth and frightening responsibility. It might be much easier to reject this doctrine altogether.

If you do, certain inevitable corollaries will follow. Without a God to bother you, you are let off. You, like the other mammals, need only worry about surviving. Moreover, like all animals, you actually have no real freedoms. You do what you do simply because your instincts, appetites, and disposition dictate what you should do. There is no higher law to obey. You do the best you can to keep alive. If there is no risk to your own survival, you may help others to live, but only if by helping others you help yourself. The whole human enterprise collapses into a "dog eat dog" world. Any radiant hope is nonsense.

The shape of your life and the life of the world will be determined by the belief you have—whether God or no-God.

I believe in Jesus Christ, true God and true man.

If you believe this, you have God coming into clear focus. No longer do you wonder what God is like, nor what he has done and will do for you. He died on a cross for you, because he loves you so. He does not stand off in his heavens, merely to judge you or observe you. He is in the thick of your sins and hurts. The guilt and the failure of man have been overcome, by God the Son. You may walk bold and fearless into the presence of God, forgiven, justified, and restored. Through the gracious intervention of Christ who has become your brother, you are an heir, a prince or princess, in the royal house of God.

This doctrine of Jesus Christ becomes the crux, the center, of your life. In and through his life, death, and resurrection, you have freedom, forgiveness, joy, and hope.

If, on the other hand, you reject this doctrine, and regard Jesus as only another of the noble people who have lived and died, you are left to struggle alone. He is a splendid example of what one life was, but only an example—and probably no more than a depressing example, since you fall so far short of his life.

Longfellow's brave lines in *The Psalm of Life,*

> Lives of great men all remind us
> We can make our lives sublime,
> And, departing, leave behind us
> Footprints on the sands of time.

can only haunt us with the futility of trying, unless—unless we believe that we are not left alone in trying, but that the Lord is within reach to help us and that despite our failures he forgives and puts us on our feet again every morning for another lap of the race.

I believe in the Holy Spirit, the holy Christian church. Confessing this, you are in fact saying that in some wonderful way, through the Word and the sacraments,

God comes with a power from heaven to draw us to him and to each other. We become a family in Christ, which is the church. The church is far more and different from all organizations, clubs, or associations. It is a kind of colony of heaven here on earth. Our membership in the church, through baptism, is more profound and far-reaching than any other membership we may have.

If we fail to believe this, our membership in the congregation becomes no more than our belonging to a club. And our work in the congregation becomes commonplace, dull, often tedious, and we may indeed drop out altogether. And why not, if the church is not peculiarly the laboratory of God?

What you *know* is important, of course. You attend schools to obtain and increase knowledge and skills.

But it is what you *believe* about God and the deep meaning of existence itself that commands you, controls you, comforts you, and sets the direction of your life. Doctrine becomes very important!

You cannot prove, nor can you always demonstrate, the truth of doctrine. But God himself is active to give you a strange certainty, if you will let him. And in that certainty you anchor your hopes for this life and for the next.

Scripture: Matthew 7:24-29

I thank you, O Lord, that the church is a teacher of doctrine, the great truths from the Scriptures. I thank you that your church has treasured these truths and that faithful people in the past have made certain that I too should know them. Help me to make them my own, and to live by them. Amen.

7

Dare We Trust Man?

Is there any hope in man, or for him? Can God overcome man's stupidity and self-centeredness and employ him for the good of the world?

The twentieth century has eroded man's confidence in himself and in his neighbor. Despite his magnificent technological triumphs, man is about ready to give up on himself. His disappointments become skepticism and finally cynicism. He has created something he cannot manage. He is tempted to sit by and wait for chaos.

He has no right to give up on himself, simply because God created him to manage this earth. And God, with his limitless resources, stands ready to help him. Man, with God at his side, is the hope of the world.

Our disenchantment with man stems, in a subtle way, from our preoccupation with the scientific method. We can measure and predict the behavior of the galaxies that whirl in space, the insects that creep on the earth, and the elements in our test tubes. These all function with fixed and immutable laws. But not man. He is given the gift of freedom, and is the one erratic and unpredictable part of creation. We cannot use the scientific method on him. We cannot know the behavior of man by measuring the behavior of the rat, despite the biological similarities.

In many of our disciplines, psychology and sociology for instance, this is precisely what we have been doing.

We have applied the same "scientific" methods to man that we have found successful with his lower cousins. The outcome has been a profound disillusionment with man and a growing melancholy about man's future.

If man is no more than a complex animal, this gloomy conclusion is inevitable. But we believe that man is created "a little lower than the angels." We believe that he belongs to a kingdom that transcends the fixed pattern of nature. We believe that he can bring to bear on the life of this earth the patterns of heaven.

We are victimized also by our modern system of mass communication. Whether by television, radio, or the press, we are more likely to hear about the failures of man than about his triumphs. Exposed as we are to "the news," it is not difficult to conclude that man cannot be trusted, and that only rarely will people rise above their own self-interest to be honest and kind. We may have friends who can be trusted to do the right thing, but we write off man in general as wicked. After all, a murder or a suicide is news; an act of integrity is probably passed over.

Our pessimism may be a reaction against an earlier optimism about man. The 19th century and the early part of the 20th pictured man as essentially good, who if he understood the good would inevitably do the good. Education would lead him out of the darkness of the past into a utopian future. Man's reason would overcome his passions. Now the pendulum has swung. Man is rather thought to be controlled by dark, irrational, and primitive drives, and his reason is but a thin veneer to cover the beast in him.

In the biblical picture of man, he is neither a beast nor an angel. Without God, he is possessed by a drag toward indifference, heartlessness, and cruelty. With God, he is captured by a pull toward righteousness, love, and hope. Each of us has both the drag and the pull.

History has striking instances of both kinds. We think of Nero and Genghis Khan and Napoleon and Hitler possessed by the drag down. We see Socrates and Paul and St. Francis and Luther and Lincoln and Bonhoeffer captured by the pull of God.

And how about the love of a father for his child, the affection of a friend for a friend, the concern of an employer for his worker, the struggle of many a leader in government for justice and equality for all? We are not without evidence that human nature can rise above selfish passions to give itself for the common good. Our communities are full of glowing examples. We have no right to give up on man.

How about the youth of our day? A few years ago the older generation, shocked by new styles in hair and clothing, was almost ready to write off the whole emerging generation as anarchists. Now, hairstyles, beards, and clothing notwithstanding, we have seen our young people turn to the Lord and to the neighbor in ways that are nothing short of exhilarating. The Spirit of the Lord is afoot among them, and we look to them with wistful hope. Perhaps their radicalism has become the radicalism of the kingdom.

Two thousand years ago another young man from Galilee made the older generation of his day uneasy. He seemed to ignore the accepted rules in favor of the higher rule of love and mercy for all. Out of fear they rejected him and crucified him. But he arose from the dead and with a few followers set in motion a tidal wave of love and righteousness and freedom and integrity that changed the world. We are in their train. We, his followers, are today the key to the hope that will always be here whenever people are touched by him.

There are massive problems in our interdependent world. God never promised a world without problems. We create them. But he is pitted against them. And he has honored us with a partnership—with him—in facing them and conquering them.

Man is not doomed to be driven helplessly here and there by the forces of heredity, environment, and bio-chemistry. We are free to defy them. Again and again the miracle has occurred. Someone has been on the way down. Suddenly, or gradually, he yields to the pull from above, and something utterly new comes into his life.

This newness, the kingdom of God, becomes a leaven, a kind of yeast that finds its way into all the structures of society—into government, into industry, into the lives of families, into the fabric of the whole world.

We have no option but to trust man. God created him in his image. He gave him a conscience. He invaded the earth with a radical rescue and a radical power in Christ. He is abroad in the Holy Spirit. The possibilities for man are limitless. God being with him, he is our hope for a better world.

Scripture: Psalm 8

We dare not sell ourselves short, O Lord. You have too much at stake with us. Help us to rely on you and then join you in bringing justice, mercy, love, joy, and hope into every area of our lives. Amen.

8

Why the Church?

In recent years we have been caught in an epidemic of criticism. We become critical of almost everything—government, schools, family life—as if everything is wrong. Some things of course are wrong, and we ought to be vigilant. But we need to remember that at no point in history has everything been right. This age may be no worse, or better, than earlier periods.

This probably is true of the church too.

Without engaging in an analysis of the church's current shortcomings, I believe we should remind ourselves of the long and continuous ministry of the Christian church in the world. It has given hope to hundreds of millions, and it does so today.

The church functions in the world in three ways. It informs, it infiltrates, and it confronts.

It *informs* the world about God. It tells the story of how God deals with the people of the world. It is the story of the Bible, climaxing in the life, death, and resurrection of Jesus.

And it is a fantastic story. Little wonder that people disbelieve it. For it tells how God singled out this tiny planet (of course there may be others) for a colony of his own. It tells how God created people to be like him, in his image, and destined him to live with him forever. Think what dignity, status, and worth this gives to people.

The story goes on to tell how God, in the wake of man's disobedience and rebellion, decided not to let him go, but to recover him at the unbelievable cost of sending his Son to become a human being, to take on himself all the sin and hurt of mankind including death, and by this cosmic maneuver to free man from the enemy and to open the doors of the eternal kingdom for him again. And it tells further how God has an ear to the cries of every one of the three billion people on earth, a direct line for each of us.

Incredible as the story is, it has had a strange power of enlisting the faith of hundreds of millions of people throughout the centuries. There is simply no explanation for this power but that the story must be the Word of God. It must be the truth about our existence and universe, a truth far beyond the reaches of telescopes and laboratories.

God has chosen to save the world by the telling of this story. He has given us no great philosophical system, no political and economic model. He has told us to go to all the world with the story, and to let the story do its miraculous work. This the church has done, century after century, and the story has lifted people from meaninglessness and despair and has changed the world. The telling of the story is still the central function of the church.

The church also *infiltrates* the world. People who are captured by the story become a kind of fifth column, a leaven and a salt, a powerful influence in all areas of life. The story makes them different. They cannot treat themselves or their neighbors the same any more. All are children of God, with the status and the rights of an eternal kingdom.

An historian once told me that he believed that every significant change for good, whether in government, industry or society in general—that every change for good could be traced back to some person or persons who had been deeply moved by the story and who, in obedience to the Lord, had set out to deal with their fellow men as if they were of such tremendous worth to God.

I have known people, and so have you, who in their daily work in business or farming or government or the professions were obviously moved to decisions and actions not in order to gain for themselves but to discharge their responsibilities of justice and mercy to people, as a duty under God. They are the salt that keeps life from rotting, the cement that holds the whole structure of society from collapsing.

Let no one ever be blind to this silent, pervading and powerful invasion of the story into the affairs of the world. And let no one limit this influence of the church for the hope of the future.

And the church *confronts* the world. It sets before the world's conscience the demands of God and humanity.

As an institution or organization it may seem slow and tardy in its movement against the ills of society. Too often it seems to conform when it ought to transform. It is important to remember that an institution will always move more slowly than its members. Your church body or your congregation may indeed fail to take a stand on some social and political issue, but this does not mean that the church (as the people of God) has been indifferent. Its members may in countless ways be involved in the struggle, and in the struggle be inspired and instructed by their church.

Two thousand years of the history of the Christian church are rich with the martyrdom of pastors and people who have confronted the powers of the world with the demands of their Lord and who have gone to their deaths because the conscience of the world could not tolerate them. The church has not been without its hours of extraordinary courage and sacrifice.

Albert Einstein, not of the Christian faith, declared that during the Nazi regime he had hoped that at least the universities or the press would stand up to the oppression of Hitler, but they capitulated. He went on to say that only one institution, the church, had the strength and boldness to do so. It is when the issue becomes "shall we obey God or man?" that the church confronts the world in a way peculiar to itself. The hope of the world is in no small way strengthened by this quality of the church. And this is not gone from our generation.

The singular mission of the church will be the telling of the story. We have an evangel, the good news, to bring. No other institution in society is charged with this task. In our country we do this voluntarily, neither controlled nor supported by government. We want it this way. And it is one of the most treasured privileges that we have—to make sure that this "old, old story of Jesus and his love" be told to our age and to the generations that follow us. Our hope for this world and the next depends on the telling.

Scripture: Matthew 16:13-20

Make me deeply grateful, O Lord, for your church. Make me aware of its weaknesses, but also make me proud of its strengths. Let me not berate it but have me be your agent to make it faithful. In both word and life, help me to be a teller of the story. Amen.

9

The Power of Waiting

There may be greater power in waiting for something than in having it. A boy is promised that on his birthday he will get a bicycle. Every day he walks by the store to gaze at it. He dreams of it. He counts the days. Then his birthday comes, and he has his bicycle. A week later his mother has to remind him to get it off the streets. He was controlled by waiting more than by possessing.

This is true not only of children. In fact, Christians are called "the children of promise." We are held fast by the promises of God, that which is yet to be. To be sure, we have ample evidences of promises fulfilled. But our hopes are attached to things yet to be, and we are held on course by those hopes. We are controlled by that which we wait for.

The tragedy would be that we tire of waiting and give up hope. Then we would be adrift. The rudder of our craft is hope, the strength is waiting.

I have always liked Rudyard Kipling, and especially his poem, *If.*

> If you can keep your head when all about you
> Are losing theirs and blaming it on you;
> If you can trust yourself when all men doubt you
> But make allowance for their doubting too;
> *If you can wait and not be tired by waiting,*

Or being lied about, don't deal in lies,
Or being hated don't give way to hating,
And yet don't look too good, nor talk too wise . . .

To become tired of waiting is to give up hope. You have met people like that. They are given to pessimism, to indifference, to drifting, perhaps even to despair. They have given up on the high art of waiting.

The Old Testament is one great epic of waiting. This little nation of Israel was buffeted between the great powers. By all the probabilities of history they should have long since been extinguished. Again and again they were swept into exile and slavery; again and again a small remnant returned to rebuild. They were kept on course by their undying ability to wait—to wait on the Lord for something he had promised. To be sure, he had delivered them from the Egyptians under the leadership of Moses. And there were other promises fulfilled. But the great fulfillment always lay in the future. God had promised, and they could wait. They are still waiting— for the Messiah—and they are still a people strangely intact through the centuries.

We believe that the end has come of waiting for the Messiah. We believe Jesus Christ is the fulfillment of that promise, and that the Savior has come. Salvation has been delivered. We revel and glory in his cross and his presence.

But we are still a "waiting" people. We wait for the consummation of the kingdom which he has already established in our midst. There will be a great day when he returns to end this sort of life, with its tragedies, its sins, its pain, its death, and when he will usher in the fulness of his kingdom.

In the meantime we are called on daily to count on him, wait on him, for the riches of life, here and now.

Waiting is not a state of inactivity or indifference. We do not simply sit by to wait. We live in a high state of expectation. A lover waits for his beloved, a father for his son returning from war, a politician for the outcome of the elections. We may in fact be more "active" when we wait than when we possess. Our friends may say, "Be patient, there's nothing you can do but wait." Patience is hard to come by. There is too much at stake. We wait with longing and yearning.

Let us not be discouraged if fear lurks around the corner. Waiting is almost always companioned by fear. The farmer who waits for his wheat to ripen has fear. He knows that wind or hail or insects could destroy the crop. Even if he has had a fine crop for fifteen successive years, the fact is that it could fail this year. Prepared as he is, the student facing his bar examinations waits the testing with as least mild anxiety.

And fear fights against faith as we wait for the fulfillment of God's promises. Faith and doubt are twins, as are trust and anxiety. Faith and trust should hold the field, of course, but fears will molest us. We would be less than human if this were not so.

A good exercise is to look back. Take inventory of the many times you have waited for something to happen, and it has happened. Or, if it did not happen, how little it mattered, really. Rather than lie awake fretting over the events of the future, start making a mental list of all the blessings which the Lord has delivered. The list can be almost endless.

The church's mission is in large part recalling us to the past, in order to strengthen us for the present and to give us hope in our waiting. We are reminded of God's care of his people in the past. He created us in love. He chose a people, Israel, and stayed by them and delivered them again and again. In the fulness of time he came in Christ Jesus to live and to die and to rise again. He would never have invaded this earth in person if he did not love us and have great plans for us. We do not wait in a vacuum. We wait in the amazing history of a God who makes and keeps promises. We would have to discount this entire history as nothing but fantasy were we to give up and not wait with hope.

I want a lot of things for myself, for my family, and for the world. I want a world at peace. I want the elemental necessities, food and shelter. I want my children and grandchildren to have a world in which they may find meaningful work to do. I try to want for myself and for others, above all else, that we grow to be like Jesus Christ and that we gladly serve him, whatever the adversities and pains of life may be. It is often difficult to have this be the highest priority in our hopes, and in our waiting. But let us try!

Scripture: Romans 8:18-28

Help us, O Lord, to want what you want for us, and then help us to count on you. We grow impatient in our waiting. You know best when we are ready to receive what our hearts desire. Help us to wait for you. Amen.

10

God and Our Country

Will God be able to use the United States to usher the world to a better future? Some historians see our country as the greatest threat to the world. Others see us as the greatest promise and hope. Our Lord said, "To whom much is given, of him shall much be required." On that basis, among all the nations of the world we bear the heaviest responsibility and face God's most frightening judgment.

For in the past two centuries no part of the world has been blessed as we.

Our founding fathers, coming from across the Atlantic, planned that on these shores would be established an ideal government, where oppression and want would never be known and where justice would exist for everyone. All would be free—free to own property, free to assemble and publish without restraint, free to choose their leaders, free to worship God according to their conscience.

Very early it was apparent that this freedom was not for all. The black people, kidnapped from Africa and regarded as little more than animals, had no freedom. The American Indians, pushed ever westward, were not free. Immigrants from southern Europe and non-Protestants had to fight their own battles for freedom.

Nonetheless, there has developed on these shores a

43

nation almost unique in the freedoms and opportunities open to a vast majority of its people. God has allowed us to be singularly blessed.

It is a frightening thing to be in command of such resources and material wealth, of such political power, and of such a heritage of freedom. Never in all the history of the world has a nation had such cause to tremble before the judgment of God. We have been given much. Of us surely much will be required. Do we have the sheer moral and spiritual strength to measure up to the demands of the hour?

Many voices in our own land, and in the world at large, will affirm that we have lost whatever high resolve we may once have had, and that we no longer can claim to be the hope of the world.

Let us not sell either God or our country short. At the risk of seeming blind to the obvious ills and shortcomings, it seems right to engage in an inventory of the "good stuff" God still has to work with in our land. There must be a case for our country playing a stellar role in projecting hope for the world.

We have immense economic and political power. To be sure, we may use these to destroy ourselves and the world. But we need not. And there certainly are signs that we are awake to the fact that our world is now so interlocked that never again can we live in isolation. Never again can we even hope to survive at the expense of other nations. We who have prided ourselves on independence now are beginning to champion a world of *interdependence*. Out of sheer self-interest, if not out of compassion for our neighbors, we have become internationalists. This itself is a sign of hope.

We may not be altogether a model for other nations, but in the very fabric of our nation are values still strong and virile that can well be emulated.

Our educational system, designed to give every child a chance of personal fulfillment and a productive place in society, still is the best in the world. It fails, to be sure, and is under continuous criticism, but never in the history of the world has a child, despite his economic and ethnic limitations, had such opportunity for receiving an education.

Our court system, cluttered and slow-moving as it sometimes becomes, is still a guarantee that the individual may receive a hearing and be judged by his peers. There are no midnight arrests by secret police and no life-long sentence of exile in some concentration camp. And throughout the maze of laws, federal, state, and local, there is the recognition that there is a higher law, a transcendent dimension of right over against which all law must ultimately be judged. Man is neither the author nor the measure of law.

Then, consider the vast voluntary enterprises of our people. We do things, not because the government or some commercial giant tells us we must, but because we want to. We build and support the work of our churches. We give money to an impressive network of causes for the common good. More and more we have capitulated to "let the government do it," but the spirit for voluntary effort is still strong.

This voluntarism is deeply imbedded in the life of Christians. I remember an old couple, renting a most modest little apartment and he earning but $19.50 a week, every week putting $1.90 in a tin cup for "the work of the Lord." And another man, more affluent, making sure that he gave away at least 30% of his income to the church and other worthy causes (the percent the government allowed as deductible). This voluntary management of money is at the heart of freedom and of our democratic society. And it is still here.

We hear much of the injustice suffered by our minorities, and without any doubt these reports are true. There are glaring injustices and inequities, inexcusable for a rich country like ours. On the other hand, in the last decade or two is there any place in the world where so much has been done for minorities in legislation, in scholarship help, and even in public attitude as in our land? There is hope.

Is there not hope too in the very openness and volume of our self-criticism? We are not disposed, as a nation, to make excuses for the years in Vietnam, the corruption of our government leaders, the violence in the streets, for the gnawing suspicion that we who are conventional and comfortable have sinned by omission. This very self-examination, inspired often by our youth, is a sign of hope.

God may still be able to use us, as a nation, to be a bridge to hope for the world. We may still be spared the awesome judgment of God and history. We have untouched resources, both in secular power and spiritual reserves, for God to employ in having us be a promise for the world's betterment.

The worst possible posture would be to give up. To escape into indifference or even cynicism is the coward's way, or the way of the man of no faith or little faith.

I love my country. I am aware of the incredible blessings God has given me and millions of people through this land. I would be ungrateful to him and faithless in my responsibility to him were I to do less than embrace a hope for this country and for the world.

Scripture: Psalm 67

Dear God, to count my blessings is to reach a point of staggering thanksgiving. And among the blessings, this

*land you have given me is among the dearest. Help
me to love my country, to see its weaknesses to be sure,
but not to discount its strengths. And let me be an agent
for its healing and for its place in the hope of the world.
Amen.*

11

Upheavals in History

On February 20, 1943, a Mexican farmer, Dionisio Pulido, saw a thin column of white smoke curling up snake-like from his field. As he went forward to investigate, he heard a muffled report. The column of smoke grew thicker and suddenly seemed to be driven skyward by a tremendous force. Then an earthquake; seismographs in New York, 2250 miles away, recorded it. Tremendous explosions, leaping tongues of flame were shooting into the sky, and masses of stone, white-hot, were being hurled a thousand feet through the air. The third day the first stream of lava belched forth, a tide 20 feet thick and 200 feet wide.

This was the birth of a volcano, the first since 1759 in the western hemisphere. One day life was routine in this farming village, but underneath in the bowels of the earth gigantic forces were building up that finally burst the earth's crust, demolished an area of 100 square miles, and dislocated 8000 people. Now the new volcano, Paricutin, 180 miles west of Mexico City, towers 1200 feet above the quiet countryside.

There are historians who think of the history of nations and of the world as huge, repetitious cycles, and conclude as the writer in Ecclesiastes, "What has been is what will be, and what has been done is what will be done; and there is nothing new under the sun." Civilizations rise and fall, each surging up and each plunging down in identical patterns of strength and weakness.

Other historians see the story of man as an ascending plateau, each successive generation inheriting the experience and wisdom of the preceding one, each rising a bit higher than its antecedents.

Still others see history as a series of upheavals, each with catastrophic power, each followed by wide-spread changes in the life of man. Life runs on in uneventful order for years. Only the most perceptive can hear the rumblings underneath the surface. Then suddenly there is eruption. The brew cannot longer be contained. Old values and traditions lose their hold, governments may topple, the seams that had held the fabric together weaken and tear, new shapes yet unformed are in the making. History is in disarray and disorder.

For a thousand years the world knew a *pax Romana*, the rule of the Roman empire. Absorbing high cultural values from its conquered peoples, Greece and others, the culture of Rome for several centuries developed a civilization of law unrivalled in the ancient world. But power turned to tyranny, and law became the plaything of the elite. In the year 408 A.D., Alaric the Goth swept down from the north and conquered the empire, by now but a shell already destroyed by its own inner corruption. And Augustine, in Africa, wrote his *City of God*, calling attention to the fact that here we have no abiding city, no lasting culture and empire.

On the wreckage of the empire, the church reared its edifice. In the disorder and chaos that ensued with the fall of political empire, the church became not only the cementing force of life but the custodians of culture through the long years called the Dark Ages. The church, almost forced to assume temporal power by the need of the times, became victim of the same temptations to aggrandizement and tyranny. And the church was never designed for this role by its Master who had told Pilate, "My kingdom is not of this world."

Then came the Renaissance. In the Middle ages nature was a closed book. But with the Crusades and with increased navigation, the West rediscovered the treasures of Greek civilization, with its concentration on nature. Medieval Christianity, in its war on the Old Adam and in its moulding of the spiritual man, had divorced man from the nature within him and from the environing world. The rediscovery of man as a child of nature released powerful creative forces which ushered in centuries of exploration of both man and his world. This prepared the ground for humanism, which has had the devastating effect of divorcing natural man from the spiritual man, and has ushered in our modern, so-called secular age.

Within the life of the church, grown more powerful and monopolistic, quiet and often unnoticed forces were fermenting which, in the opening of the 16th century, catapulted Christendom into a catastrophic period known as the Reformation. These forces, deeply spiritual, broke up the visible oneness of the church, created new centers of ecclesiastical power, and introduced the age of pluralism in the life of the church.

Any study of history will reveal much the same pattern. Forces and movements are afoot, at first scarcely noticed and initially regarded as non-revolutionary, which gather momentum and, either suddenly or gradually, usher in a whole new age.

With the advent of science we now have moved swiftly to the dominion and often tyranny of the machine. With Nietzsche and Marx, humanism, with its free play of exuberant human creative energy, is already discredited. In its place there is the uneasy urge to establish some sort of communal and compulsory life through govern-ment. Man, left to himself without God, has lost faith in himself and may be becoming the slave of the machine he has created.

What upheavals are we witnessing now? What silent and unidentified forces are even now brewing which may alter radically the life of our grandchildren?

We speak rather openly about the lurking power of the atom, the rising tide of the non-white people of the world, the depletion of food and energy for the world, the revolution of woman against man, the decline of democratic governments. And we ask anxiously, will the family survive, will there be jobs and personal fulfill-ment, will the church live?

No one dares to take these issues lightly. History is indeed in the making, and what we may have to suffer or endure or enjoy, we cannot know. God only knows.

One thing is certain. If man cannot or will not conceive of himself as a child of God as well as a child of nature, there can be little hope. Without God man will give up. Only as a child of God will he claim and exercise the kind of freedom, responsibility, and accountability that can carry us through history's upheavals to shape the new forms into instruments for the good of man.

The church, therefore, has a pivotal role. It must call men back to God, to stand under him in judgment, and to be empowered by his mercy. God may create the upheavals. He assuredly can see us through them. Whether they are produced by evil forces or good, he can use them for our good if we but let him. In him there is always hope.

Scripture: 1 Peter 3:8-12

You are the Lord of history, we know, but we also know that history is often shaped by the sinfulness of men.

Help us to see our responsibilities under you, and help each of us to discharge these duties conscientiously. Let us never forget that we are children of yours, and that our fulfillment lies in doing your will. Amen.

12

Providence

A bee flew in through the open window. The man laid down his morning newspaper and watched, fascinated by the bee's frantic attempts to find its way out again. It dashed its little body against one window pane after another, missing the one open space and becoming more frantic with each frustrating attempt.

The man picked up a towel and tried to guide the bee's flight toward freedom. But the bee, regarding him and the towel as the foe, hurled itself against the towel and buzzed about the room in panic. At long last the man succeeded in maneuvering the creature to the open window and suddenly the bee, sensing the sunshine and trees, flew into the wide open world to which it belonged.

Does God use circumstances which we regard as hostile like that? And do we, misunderstanding the ways of Providence, resist and struggle against the very things that are guiding us to health and freedom?

In retrospect we may be able to understand. The loss of a job, defeat in an election, disappointment in love, even sickness—looking back, we are able to see that each adversity was the closing of a door which drove us to seek other doors, and that the door or doors which finally opened to us led to unexpected advantage and blessing.

We may regard this closing and opening of doors as

mere coincidence, as chance. Or we may believe that God himself has something to do with guiding our ways.

A man misses a plane connection by minutes. The next flight will not be in time for his daughter's birthday party. Sitting in the lounge dejected, his ears catch an emergency news release. There has been a plane crash, and it is the flight he would have taken had he made it on time. Coincidence? Most likely, but he thanks God for having closed this door and given him another chance at life.

Even if we believe that God protects us from danger and harm, we cannot conclude that he has designed and arranged everything that happens to us. This kind of religious determinism or fatalism will not do justice to God or to our own right to choose. It would likely be of small comfort to the distraught parents whose little girl had been killed by a drunken driver to be told "God knows best," as if God had arranged for the man to get drunk in order to execute some great benevolent plan for their little girl.

To believe, however, that God can take even this tragedy and misfortune and use it as a door to lead father and mother to a new appreciation of life itself, to a fresh discovery of their love for each other and their need of each other, and to gratitude for the three years they had had with their little girl, this kind of dividend is God's way of having new doors open.

If we believe that God is in the midst of things that happen, then we also must believe that he does not let evil go unpunished. He has put this universe together in such a way that "what we sow, that shall we reap." Evil has a way of catching up with itself. It carries the seed of its own destruction.

It may be difficult to believe this. Wicked and ruthless people seem to get by. They become rich and powerful, when people who are honest and kind are pushed aside. But there are rewards and punishments not easily seen. What of the uneasy conscience, the gnawing fears of discovery, the continuing need for pretense and hypocrisy that plague the inner man, the built-in punishment for wickedness? And what of the peace of mind which rewards those who pursue honesty and justice?

In the providence of God, evil is not only overcome by good, but evil destroys evil. A dishonest public official who becomes wealthy on bribes and extortion, for instance, becomes the envy of other dishonest men who covet his ill-gotten gains and who then plot his destruction. Destroying him, they in turn become candidates for this same wretched sequence of destruction. Nations that lust for power are overcome by other nations that lust for power.

While there is scant comfort in thinking of history as the grim story of one evil man destroying another evil man, nonetheless there is some reassurance in the fact that forces for good can at times find strange alignment with evil itself in a righteous cause. An old catechism poses the question, "How does God deal with man in his sinfulness?" and gives this answer, "God allows him to sin, but he sets limits to his sins." And these limits are, in God's providence, not only those that come from good opposing evil but also from evil destroying itself.

God has given freedom to man. The puzzle is that with man's flagrant abuse of this freedom God does not take it away from him. Why doesn't he fire him from the management of life, reduce him to a puppet, and once and for all prevent us from having wars and oppression and injustice? But he doesn't. He keeps us on the job, even at the risk of having us use our freedoms for evil.

The only answer—and it's a strange one—is that we are God's children and that he loves us. To remove our freedoms would be to put us all in cages in some kind of zoo. And he does not want a zoo; he wants a family.

And we are his family, all three billion of us, good children and bad, children who love him and obey him and children who have fled him to the far country and who may be separated from him forever. He has not exiled us to this island called earth and left us to our own devices. He is on the island, in the thick of things. He judges and punishes, he guides and rewards. He commands and he persuades.

Most of all, he persuades in love. The cross is the supreme evidence of his way with us. To persuade us to abandon our self-centered and sinful ways, he sent his only Son to become one of us and to die for us.

But the cross is more than an eloquent plea for our love and faithfulness. It is in fact God's way of overcoming the prince of evil, the devil, who is at the heart of our disobedience. It is God's way of opening the door of his kingdom to us. It is his way of being in the very center of the struggle between good and evil.

The outcome of the struggle is settled. Caught as we are in the fight within our own hearts, and caught as we are in the ebb and flow of good and evil in our world, there is no question what the eventual victory will be. Good will triumph. This does not mean that in this world of time good will gradually overcome evil and our remote descendents will know a society in which all the ills are gone. It does mean that a final judgment will, in God's own way, destroy evil and have good hold the field forever.

In Christ Jesus, God the Son, our brother and Lord and Savior, we who until death will at times be overcome by our own evil and the evil of the world, we can through his grace rest secure in this ultimate triumph.

Scripture: Psalm 23

I thank you, O God, that you have not left us to ourselves on this earth, but that you work out your good for us in all the circumstances of life. Let me not judge every disappointment as evil, and even in those that are tragedies let me look for doors to good that you may open for me. Amen.

13

I Don't Need to Live

Hanns Lilje, later bishop of Hannover and president of the Lutheran World Federation, baffled his interrogator in the Nazi prison. Again and again this Hitler official tried to break him. Threatening him with death, and hearing Lilje's calm reply, "But I don't need to live," the interrogator sat speechless. What sort of man was this who did not need to live?

Is there not a profound sense in which every Christian who has "died with Christ" and who has lost his life to Christ should be able to join Lilje? The apostle Paul, saying farewell to his friends in Ephesus, said, "I am going to Jerusalem. . . . Imprisonment and afflictions await me. But I do not account my life of any value nor as precious to myself, if only I may accomplish my course and the ministry which I received from the Lord Jesus, to testify to the gospel of the grace of God." Luther, facing the hostile powers of the church and empire at Worms, knew that he could lose his life in refusing to capitulate and recant, but said, "Here I stand, I can do no other."

You and I may not have reached the strength of a Lilje, a Paul, or a Luther. But if we belong to Christ at all, must we not be on the way? Is there not one need, and one alone that pushes all other needs aside—the need to be faithful to our Lord? We should be on the way to dying to all other needs.

And what does this overall death to self mean? Dare we have any needs, any hope, other than to belong to Christ and to be faithful to him?

Dare we hope for a world at peace, a world where hunger and disease are gone? Dare we hope personally for health, a good job, friends, a contented family, acceptance from our peers, a long life?

The answer is probably self-evident. Yes, we may entertain these hopes if (and it is a big *if*) they do not deflect us from the one thing needful. They may even become needs, if as needs they do not become so fixed and absolute that we cannot let them go.

After all, these hopes and needs may, or may not, be realized. Every one may elude us. There may be no world at peace, no world without hunger. Our health, our job, our friends, our family, our approval from others—all this may go. If we have allowed any one of them, or all of them together, to become so strong that they possess us, then when they go, we are gone. We are undone. Life falls apart for us. We allowed the wrong things to be at the center of our needs and hopes, and when the center is gone, we fall apart and are destroyed.

There is only one safeguard. We must have but one towering, central and absolute need—to be in Christ and to be faithful to him. This is *the need;* all else are but the luxuries, the side issues of life. Health may come or go, but the center is secure. Even life may go, but the center is safe. Neither life nor death can separate us from the love of God in Christ.

It may be easy for me to write these words and easy for you to read them. But to live this life is another matter. It means a sort of freedom that faces both death and fate with a strange looseness, a divine nonchalance.

A person wants very much to get a certain job. He uses every honorable way to get it. All the while he says to himself, "I don't need that job." If he loses, his center is still secure. He wanted it, he hoped for it, but he did not need it. His profound need had been met in having his life rest in God, come what may.

A man is ambitious. He wants money and power. And he succeeds. But he is a Christian. The center of his being is hid with Christ. Now, neither money nor power possess him. He swings free with these achievements or gifts. He lets them go, he uses them for the good of others. They become these accidental dividends that he returns to God. And should he lose them all and be in poverty, no matter. They were never at the center. He really never needed them.

It becomes more difficult in things that matter most, a happy and contented family life, for instance. Despite our best efforts (or perhaps because of our neglects), the family falls apart. Mother and father are separated, and children shuffle between them for love and security. The loss may threaten to destroy some of the fondest hopes. It will be much harder to say, "I did not need family," but even this is possible if lives find refuge in the central love and forgiveness of God.

We fight for life. Survival is an elemental drive in each of us. Jesus warned, "Whoever seeks to gain his life will lose it, but whoever loses his life will preserve it." Even life itself is to be held tentatively, in an open hand, as if we are ready to let it go. And there are stakes so high that we must be ready to die, rather than lose the prize. Lilje knew it, and Paul. And even in this modern day, thousands have gone to their deaths rather than jeopardize the one thing needful.

Most of us will not likely have a dramatic test, like Luther. But life will be filled with "little deaths." My claim to comfort must die in the face of another's hurt. My right to justice must be surrendered because of someone's need for mercy. My need for acceptance must die because the price of acceptance is to lie or to fawn. Each little death will help us understand better what the big death is, our death to all but our life with God.

What freedom there is in saying, "I desire them, I work for them, I hope for them, but I don't need them. There is but one thing needful, and in Christ Jesus I have that." Gone is this petty competition for advantage and gain; gone is the need to defend my rights; gone is any peevishness over the ingratitude of others; gone is the paralysis of hopes unrealized; gone is even the need to be loved in return for love. We rise above the jungle of the foothills of life and have the serene vision of the mountain heights.

This dying is not a once-and-for-all event. It is a lifelong struggle. We die daily. Needs that ultimately are relative and even unworthy will rear their heads to make their claims. Again and again the Holy Spirit will have to help us usher them into their proper, lower places. The throne belongs to the one great need, our life with God.

This demoting of desires and hopes to their proper places will not be without pain. But the pain will finally be the greater if we allow them to usurp the throne. We will lose our souls to the usurpers.

We will find ourselves, our brothers and sisters, our world, and God as we are captured by the one central need and this alone. I do not need to live. I have God, and God has me.

Scripture: Luke 10:38-42

Dear God, let me not be so fastened to even my fondest hopes that I forget that life with you is finally the one thing needful. And with my life hid in Christ, keep all desires, needs, and hopes from taking control of my life. At the same time, thank you for letting me have soaring hopes for my life and for your children the world over. Amen.

14

The Bible:
Book of Hope

For some people, the Bible is largely literature. It has stories, it has poetry, it has allegory and parable. Anyone presuming to be educated will take the Bible seriously as containing some of the great writings of all time.

For others, the Bible is history. It zeros in on a small nation in Asia Minor, the Israelites, and chronicles their long and turbulent relationships with other nations. And in the New Testament it centers on the career of a young carpenter from Nazareth and the later history of his followers.

For still others, it is a book of exalted spiritual and ethical insights. It is a book of instruction for people who take seriously the search for values. It takes its place in the world's library of moral classics.

For many it is the record of man's search for God. It tells how people think they have found him. They found him in their escape from Egyptian oppression, in their conquest of "the promised land," in their repeated return to Jerusalem after periodic exile. And, in the New Testament they found him in Jesus Christ as the Messiah.

But for us the book is more than literature, more than history, more than moral instruction, more than an account of man's search.

We believe that it is strangely a book in which and through which God is in search of man.

The ancient Scandinavians had a legend about a *Black Book*, a book with black pages and the writing in blood, the devil's book. If anyone opened its pages to read, they would be possessed. The devil would leap out from the pages to take the reader captive.

As a sublime parallel, the Bible is God's book. It is the vehicle which conveys God to man. It is the cradle in which we find the Lord and the Lord finds us. By the power of the Holy Spirit, God leaps out from its pages to dwell in us and with us. It is a book of strange power.

It is also a very human book. It did not drop down from heaven fully edited by God and his angelic secretaries. It reflects all the qualities of a purely human document. And scholars, believing that it is just that and no more, find it an eminently rich and fascinating book. The writers were people, some history-writers, some poets, some teachers. And they wrote as they did in the context of their own day. They probably did not think they were different from other writers.

But we believe that they were moved or inspired by God to write as they did. We believe God used them in his search for man. We believe, therefore, that the book has a strange power, unlike other books. For us it is an altogether unique book.

We do not believe that God's purpose with the writers or the book was to convey historical or scientific facts, however. He has other ways of letting us in on the secrets of his universe and the data of history. The Bible is not an encyclopedia of knowledge. The biblical writers thought that the world was flat, but that was before God used Copernicus and the space age to show us that the world is round. No one would go to the Bible to find out what God has to say about dogs or stars, for instance; God has other ways of teaching us about dogs and stars.

But there simply is no other way for God to reveal his love for us. The wheeling planets don't tell us that he loves us, however much we know about planets. The incredible ecological balance of nature only tells us that God is a God of order. It is in the Bible alone that we have the promise and the record of his love. "God spoke to our fathers by the prophets; but in these last days he has spoken to us by a Son." God has broken silence. He has let himself be known. Supremely in Jesus Christ he has given us the guarantee of that love.

If we will take the Bible seriously, in faith, and believe that God is trying to reach us with his truth and with his love through this book, then the book becomes for us a powerful record of his love in the past and an equally powerful promise of his love for today and for tomorrow.

Love is more than an attitude in the heart of God. He does not sit behind some fleecy cloud wishing us well. Love bursts into action. And the Bible is a record of the mighty acts of God for us. The very fact that he bothered to create us is evidence of his love. Then go on to read how with infinite patience he executed his plan to recover us from the bondage of the Fall, how he chose Abraham, how he singled out a small nation and groomed them for the coming of the Savior, how he rescued them from the Pharaoh and led them through the wilderness, how he sent them the prophets and how, in the fulness of time, he sent his Son to die for us.

The Bible goes on to assure us that God already has such a stake in us that he surely will not drop us. He who has begun this good work in us and for us will see it through. He wants us with him throughout eternity, and nothing less will do.

In the meantime he still has us out on this island of his called earth. This is no penal colony where he punishes us with pain and sorrow and tragedy until he thinks we've had enough. He has great plans for this island and its life. His kingdom is here too, as well as in heaven. And we, through holy baptism, have been ushered into this kingdom.

Our Lord taught us specifically to pray, "Thy kingdom come; thy will be done on earth as it is in heaven." He would never have had us pray this prayer if he did not hold out hope that this could happen. The earth is a place where the glories of his kingdom can be reflected in all the areas of life.

The Bible really becomes the book of the kingdom, a bridge between heaven and earth. It is the book of history and instruction; it is above all the book of promise and of hope.

God cannot use it very well if it lies unopened on your end table. You will need to open it and read. You will read it best if you do not expect to find in it all the answers to life's mysteries. Read it to find God, or better still, to let God find you. Expect him to steal into your heart. He will disturb you, but he comes primarily with love and comfort and peace and hope.

God will use some parts of the Bible more effectively than others. You cannot expect the long genealogies in Numbers to capture you as, for instance, the Twenty-third Psalm or the Gospel of John. But in every one of the 66 books of the Bible you will find something which will stir your mind and heart and send your spirit soaring in hope.

The Bible has inspired many other books, books that vibrate with hope. But these are all little streams that flow out from the great spring, the book of books. We have the high privilege of drinking from its waters— and live!

I neglect your Book again and again, O Lord, and thus rob myself of the hope that surges through it. Help me to search its pages, and then keep surprising me with your presence in it, and from it into my heart. I need its assurance of your past blessings, and I need its promises for my tomorrows. Amen.

15

These Crippling Moods

As a Christian I believe I am free to make choices. This freedom is given me both at creation and again in redemption. I am not a pawn to be pushed here and there. Even God does not push me. He respects my right to choose, even when I choose evil.

He has honored me with joint management of the earth—with him. By the use of my freedom I shape history and the future, for good or ill. I am given responsibility and will be held accountable.

All sorts of forces, some rational, some irrational, tempt me to irresponsibility and to moods of hoplessness. But for the Christian the only valid mood is hope. God has given us an open future, with his own grand fulfillment at the end. In the meantime, because we use our freedoms for evil as well as for good, our history and the world's history will have their dark and tragic underside. At times it will seem that there is nothing but tragedy, with death at the end.

All of us are given to moods. They come and go. If God is left out of our reckoning, all our moods will tend to demobilize us for any courage, even for any effort in the struggle.

I describe these various moods as pessimism, skepticism, indifference, optimism, cynicism, and despair.

In my moments of pessimism, I tend to see only the dark side. I recognize that man may choose, but dominated by self-interest his choices always tend away from the good. Or I may conclude that he is no more than "a helpless piece of the game" which blind fate keeps tossing about with no pattern or design. I see nothing but disaster and catastrophe for him in his future.

On a slightly brighter side, I may only be skeptical. I have grave doubts. I see man as capable of both good and evil, but I have my grave misgivings about the good ever holding the field. I survey the historical scene with a critical eye, as indeed I should, and I conclude that the past is predominantly a record of man's failures. And my doubts get in the way of any concerted effort for betterment. I simply cannot muster any gallantry, any boldness, any hope.

Indifference is a mood more common, and ultimately more damaging, than any other. This really presupposes that nothing matters. The universe itself is indifferent. It makes no distinction between good and evil, right or wrong. It has no purpose or destiny for man. We are but accidents of biology that "strut and fret our hour upon the stage" and then disappear into the nothingness from which we came. Why bother with anything, except perhaps to avoid pain and pillage a bit of pleasure these few swift years we have upon the earth?

We applaud optimism as a good mood, but it has its dangers for the struggle. If our optimism is based on the belief that man is essentially good, that his failures are only a bit of mischief, that everything will turn out well "in the wash," then this rosy-hued outlook may be as treacherous as pessimism. Why bother to fight if the battle is not a serious one, and if the future will largely take care of itself and rather automatically usher us into the better day? Optimism, as commonly understood, is not the same as Christian hope.

Cynicism is skepticism gone sour. A highly intelligent and reflective mind is most susceptible to this mood. It also is a dominant mood of our day. Only a century ago the intelligentsia of our western civilization wrote extensively of a new day dawning in the world's history. Man had evolved from his more primitive and brutal past to let reason take control. Education was the key. When man reached the point—and he was rapidly getting there—where he understood that war, for instance, could not solve his problems, he would no longer fight wars. Then came two World Wars, fought by the most reflective and highly civilized of the nations. And a profound cynicism crept into our western world. We are now tempted to believe that reason is but a thin veneer that camouflages the irrational, passionate, and primitive drives that constitute the dynamics of man's behavior. And that the future is plunging on to catastrophe.

Cynicism, if it is not rescued by a renewal of Christian hope, will sink into the dark and static mood of despair, sometimes called nihilism. This is darker than pessimism, more fierce than indifference. Despair embraces the nothingness of life with a kind of abandon. The end is the cataract and the abyss, and our craft is sweeping down the surging rapids relentlessly. The oars are gone and we hear the thunder of the waterfall. The best we can do in the moments that remain is to wolf down what food we have, drain the bottle, and fornicate as we may. Nothingness yawns to receive us.

Any one of these moods is destructive, and unworthy of the Christian. Each is in its way a cop-out from the magnificent campaign of the kingdom of God on earth.

God is here, in the thick of the fight. Every human being is a "military objective" of eternal value. Every concrete situation that we face has eternal issues lurking within it. Right and wrong, good and evil, righteousness and unrighteousness are real alternatives. Justice, mercy, purity, and integrity are real values. The earth is the Lord's, a sector of his empire, where the warfare between God and Satan is raging.

The ultimate outcome is in God's hands. Christ settled that on a cross two thousand years ago. But the kind of life we will have on this island during this interim before Christ comes again to judge and to fulfill—this kind of life is in our hands. God is at our side and in the battle, but he does not let us off. We have been commissioned. We have instructions for the campaign. We have freedom to carry on, and we have power.

We will blunder, we will stumble, we will quake with fear. At times we will retreat and run for cover. But we remember that the battle is not ours alone; it is the Lord's. The catastrophes which our sins and disobedience may bring to us personally and to the world may at times be overwhelming. These we will be called on to endure as virtually inevitable in a war of such celestial dimensions as this.

Each of us has a big sector. My family, my church, my country, my business or profession—each arena is my battleground. My performance may, or may not, have any direct bearing on what happens in Moscow or Geneva or what the 21st century may hold. But who knows? Only God knows what my faithfulness or unfaithfulness may mean for the overall war. I need not know. I need only be vigilant that no mood or circumstance weaken me for the assignment he has given me in his kingdom.

Scripture: 2 Corinthians 6:1-10

I cannot always control my moods, O Lord, but help me not to be controlled by them. The state of the world gets me down, and so does my own performance. Whatever I may feel at the moment, give me the stubborn assurance that you have a great, overall plan for me and for the world. Amen.

16

Knowledge
and Hope

I *know* that the world is round, and I *believe* that God created the world. Knowing and believing are different. I know that Jesus of Nazareth died on a cross; I believe his death was an atonement for the sins of the world. I know that people die; I believe that there is life after death.

The truth that comes through knowledge is available to everyone; the truth that comes through believing is available only to people of faith, those who believe.

In most of these chapters we talk about the hope that comes through faith. In this chapter we will try to determine whether knowledge, too, is God's way of giving us hope.

Your friend is sick and you say, "I hope he gets well." In projecting this hope you rely heavily on the medical knowledge available to the doctors and nurses. And because of the extraordinary progress in the healing sciences you have more reason for your hopes being realized today than a century ago. Or someone is flying home and we say, "We hope he will arrive safely." Again our hopes are strengthened by the amazing statistical record of safety which the airlines have. In these respects, our hopes attach themselves to knowledge.

In our hope for the good life on the earth, however,

we may conclude that the explosion of knowledge of the past century may actually diminish our prospects for the future. What of our knowledge of atomic energy? Will we blow up our cities? What about our knowledge of motors? Will we not pollute the atmosphere and make the planet uninhabitable? What about automation? Will we not create vast unemployment and social chaos?

It is probably safe to say that the massive increase of scientific and technological knowledge has not increased our hopes for the world. In fact we may fear this knowledge more than we applaud it. But should we?

Must we not believe that all knowledge comes from God? Did he not put all these wonderful resources in his universe, and did he not give man the kind of probing mind to ferret out their secrets? The alternative would be to conclude that the devil, or some mischievous spirit, had hidden these things in the universe and had beguiled man to find them, and with them to destroy himself.

I think of a father playing a game with his children. He hides all sorts of things in the living room, then summons his children to the game of finding what he has hidden. Seating himself in a chair to observe his children's search, must he not be pleased every time a child uncovers something?

I think God is like that. Many of the things he has placed in his universe are such that if improperly used they can harm. On the other hand, properly used, they can be of immeasurable good.

To be sure, man has not yet demonstrated that he can manage these marvelous resources. The release of the atom, for instance, holding such amazing promise for the world's energy needs, made possible a Hiroshima and Nagasaki, and launched the nations of the world on a wasteful race in arms. The airplane, so useful in transporting emergency medicines and food and professional help, made possible the destruction of European cities and countless lives.

On the other hand, think of the sheer drudgery that has been removed from our lives—on farms and in factories. Think of the innumerable lives that have been saved by the conquest of disease. Think of the increased knowledge in agriculture to feed the world's growing population.

It simply is not fair to God nor to technology to conclude that knowledge increases hoplessness. Knowledge should be another source of hope. Every person who works with microscopes and computers should have a right to believe that he is on God's side working for the betterment of man.

The principle given by Jesus, "To whom much is given, of him much will be required," brings our age under sober judgment. Knowledge is power. It must be used not for gain but for the common good. A nation possessing knowledge has no right to use it to aggrandize, or to overcome other nations. Under God, the nation must manage it for the good of all nations. A person who has knowledge owes his knowledge to all who don't have it and who need it. If we regard all things, including knowledge, as gifts from God, then we must conclude that they should be used as God wants them used.

A teacher, for instance, must transmit her knowledge to her students, not because she is paid a salary (she of course deserves reasonable compensation), but simply because she has the knowledge that they need. A doctor, similarly, provides medical services not because he is paid (he deserves a reasonable fee, of course), but because he has knowledge and skills which people need.

How enraged we would be if a scientist were to discover a cure for cancer and refuse to part with this knowledge unless he were paid a billion dollars for it. We would all say that quite apart from any fee, the fact that he had the knowledge obligated him to give it to all who did not have it.

Knowledge becomes a hope when it is employed for the good of all, when it is not hoarded for the exclusive use of those who have it, and when it comes under the control of love.

I confess to a sense of bewilderment over the rapidly expanding horizons of knowledge. Every new discovery creates new options. I must decide how it should be used. We are on the threshold of a new management of life itself. Long before the birth of a child, for instance, our knowledge may enable us to determine his qualities and to vote for him or against him.

Using all the spiritual and moral insights that our Christian faith gives us, we will be compelled to make many new kinds of decisions. This will not be easy. But if we believe that this expansion of knowledge is from God, we dare not throw up our hands in fear and confusion.

Within the broad and inclusive command of our Lord to love one another as he has loved us, we will make the difficult decisions that confront us in every concrete situation of life. My decision may not always be the same as yours, but if we both approach the choice out of love for God and our neighbor, we will find the way.

God has not left us at sea, after all. He has revealed himself in the Holy Scriptures and supremely in Jesus Christ. And in the long history of the church, the values that the people of God have discovered and embraced these centuries will help to guide us.

Knowledge has been a blessing, despite its misuse. It is of God. And God will not leave us without guidance and strength as we seek to use it for him and for one another. Knowledge can be hope.

Scripture: Deuteronomy 8

Must we not conclude, O God, that you give knowledge as one of your many gifts? With this gift, you multiply the choices we must make. We rely on you to give to us and to the nations of the world both the wisdom and the will to employ knowledge for your glory and for our hope. Help us. Amen.

17

The Gift of Laughter

Only man can laugh. Animals don't, or birds, or fish. To man alone did God give the gift of laughter.

If he gave it, he must intend that we use it. But isn't life too serious a business? Dare we laugh at all in the face of war, corruption, violence, pollution, and our own private sins? Isn't weeping rather the quality that makes us human?

But laughter is not of the devil; it is of God.

It is said that our age has lost its sense of humor. Laughter, except in some bizarre and lewd sense, is gone from our lives. We are engulfed by melancholy and pessimism. Most of our TV shows, designed to have us laugh, seem forced and artificial. Their distorted themes of sex and violence may elicit an uneasy chuckle, but we quickly slip back into a mood of sadness. There is no Mark Twain or Will Rogers to combine charity and humor in having us laugh at ourselves.

The Christian should have a better chance to laugh than any other. If the gift is from God, then it follows that the person who lives with God ought to have a right and a duty to employ the gift. And we do. It is when we understand and remember how God deals with man, in judgment and mercy, that we can laugh at ourselves and even at our world.

Don't misunderstand me. The Christian also has a more

profound sense of the tragedy of life than others. But the Christian has a faith to deal with tragedy. It need not be the last word about ourselves or about our world. God has intervened. He himself, supremely in Christ, has plunged into the world's tragedy.

Tragedy and comedy are two sides of the same coin. Looked at from one side we weep, looked at from the other side we laugh. There is a great gap between what we ought to be and what we are, or between what we pretend to be and what we are. When we pretend to be what we are not, we are both tragic figures and comic characters. Looking at ourselves and the gap, we may weep or we may laugh.

For instance, you see a drunken man embracing a telephone pole, caressing it and speaking endearingly to it. Your first reaction is to chuckle. You see the gap, between what he is and what he pretends to be or what he ought to be. Coming closer, you see that he is your husband or son or father. Now you stop chuckling. The gap is not comedy, it is tragedy.

In one way or another, most of us pretend to be what we are not, and to that extent we are both tragic and comic. A man succeeds in life. With a bit of luck and hard work (of course his brains and health are given him from God), he becomes a somebody. He has money and station. He becomes priggish and proud. He drops his old friends and joins the clubs. He becomes patronizing and condescending, parading this as kindness. He is a tragic figure. He is a clown. At any moment cancer could bring him down, or his brain could slip a cog.

What a great thing it would be if he could accept his good fortune with a sense of humor, guard against pride, and remain a humble recipient of God's blessings.

God created man in his image. As such, man has unlimited expectations for good. But man fell from God, separated from him. Now he has unlimited possibilities for evil. Each of us, returned to God through Christ, has the possibilities for great good. But each of us, even when restored to God, carries with him the cargo of "the old man" and may be guilty of a great gap between what we ought to be and what we are. Failing to recognize this gap, we slip into all sorts of ridiculous pretenses.

It is possible to weep over these gaps and at the same time to laugh at them—because God in his mercy through Christ has come to terms with the gap. Through the forgiveness of sin, we are regarded by God as if we have no sin at all. Christ has bridged the gap. That which we ought to be—that we *are*, by grace through faith. The gap is still there, to be sure. We fall far short every day. And the gap is tragic. But we can now chuckle too. We can laugh at ourselves. Repentance itself, which is the awareness of the gap and a will to correct what we can, can be in the context of humor.

It is almost as is Christ were to say, "You are a sinner, to be sure, and you deserve punishment, even eternal condemnation. But remember, I died on a cross to remove your sins, to bridge the gap. I have forgiven your sins and I have forgotten them. Now you laugh them off. Stop your weeping and your grovelling. Accept the gift of joy and merriment that I want you to have. And next time you face your sins, as indeed you will until you die because you will fail me again and again, be sure to remember in your repentance that I have given you the right to laugh at yourself, and to make merry with me now and throughout eternity."

Until we die we will have cause to weep over our sins, but because Christ has taken care of the gap we also have the right to the gift of humor and laughter. And the laughter will not be the raucous cackle of the world but laughter that springs from the deep wells of joy from

God himself who, despite the gap, claims us as his own.

The 20th century has seen a growing disillusionment over man's possibilities for good. The pendulum has swung from the optimistic 19th century which regarded man as basically good, needing only a bit more knowledge to close the gap for and by himself. This optimism was not from the Bible, which has always faced man's deep selfishness and his inability to close the gap. And because of this disenchantment with man, we have slipped into a pessimism that robs us of laughter and hope, and threatens us with paralysis for any noble effort or end.

Only a return to God, and to God's view of man, will restore for us the gift of both laughter and hope. Strangely, God gives us back the sense of humor and the gift of laughter at the foot of the cross.

Did Jesus laugh? I think he did. It must have been with a twinkle in his eye that he watched the people scrambling for the best seats at the banquet and advised them to take the lower seats at the start so that in the rearranging they could only move upward. He saw man pretending to be something, and saw the pretense as funny. And another time when he noted that the host had invited all his rich relatives and prominent people, he suggested that the next time he invite the poor, the blind, and the lame, who could not invite him in return. It must have been with a touch of humor that he made this observation to the host. He saw the gap, tragic but also comic.

In Psalm 2, the writer describes the plans of the rulers of the earth to dislodge God, and observes, "God, in his heavens, will laugh." He regards the pretenses of man as comedy, as well as tragedy.

He has the gift of laughter himself, and he has given it to us. It would be a pity if we, his own, did not claim it.

Scripture: Psalm 2

Let me not forget the seriousness of life, O God. But having been claimed as your child through Christ, let me not neglect the joy and merriment and laughter which you want your family to have. Teach me that tragedy and comedy have common roots, and that tears and laughter belong together for the children of God. Amen.

18

Dealing with Loneliness

Loneliness is an enemy of hope. Man was never intended to go it alone. If he does, he most likely will never know the warmth of love or the sweep of hope.

I need not be marooned on an island to be lonely. I may be elbowing my way through a crowded bus depot. I may be living in a massive apartment complex. I may be darting from class to class at a university. I am in the thick of people I don't know and who don't care. And I am lonely.

We belong to God and to one another. If we are robbed of either or both of these, we become as separate bits of debris aimlessly adrift on a turbulent stream. And it doesn't much matter where to go.

Above all, it is God who has claimed us. He wants to be father, brother, friend to us. We have people giving simple testimony that when Jesus really came into their hearts, loneliness was gone. We sing, "What a friend we have in Jesus," and in these words we express both confidence and hope. Having God, we never need to be alone. He is a powerful and invisible presence. We can speak to him in prayer and praise as we would speak to someone across the table.

But God does not give us himself alone. He gives us one another. In one sense we may have God as a warm, personal companion—him and him alone. In a deeper sense, we may never have him to ourselves, one to one. He comes to us, but he brings his family with him. And all people are his family, for he made us all. He is not satisfied that we know him alone. He wants us to know our brothers and sisters, and to belong to one another.

Think what it means to be able to share with God and with one another our hopes, our dreams, our fears, our sorrows, and our joys. This is God's will for us. Realizing this comradeship, even in part, we have gone a long way in overcoming loneliness. I will still have moments of loneliness, because I cannot altogether pierce the veil that separates me from the God who is both revealed and hidden. And no two people, however close and friendly, can penetrate the deepest recesses of the other.

But we have every right to work at it. Not until death releases us and we are fully joined with God and with one another in heaven will loneliness be totally gone. In the meantime God himself becomes a kind of usher to lead us to himself and to one another.

He ushers us into families—father, mother, brother, sister. The home becomes a laboratory in which we learn to exercise together the wonderful qualities of love and patience and faith and hope. Here we face the enemies of life not in a lonely guerilla warfare but as a united phalanx. Most of us are unaware of the strength that we have. Sometimes it takes a major tragedy or sorrow to weld us together in sympathy and hope.

Unlike our earlier pioneer days when families worked and played together, today's mobility makes it necessary for families to *work* at being together. Every effort to share life, even when miles and schedules separate us, is eminently worthwhile. A letter, a telehone call, a quick visit, and continuous prayer for one another will help. God has given us one another, in family, and it is one of his dearest gifts.

And he gives us friends, as a sort of extension to the family. The secret of having friends is invariably that I set out to be a friend—not in order to enlist friends in return, but simply to be a friend. The Samaritan in Jesus' parable did not know the poor fellow in the ditch, nor perhaps did his friendly act result in either acquaintance-ship or long friendship, but in his very act of friendship the Samaritan dealt a decisive blow to loneliness.

God also has given me a country. I am a citizen. When abroad, I carry a passport. It is my guarantee that I belong. I rest back in the strength of a whole nation, with its vast resources. Not until I left these shores and traveled in foreign lands did I feel the exhilaration of country. I can sing, "This is my country" with more profound gratitude than before.

And, like it or not, God gives me the whole human family. Everyone, irrespective of color or creed, is my brother or sister. All of us have been created by the same good God, and all of us have been redeemed at the same incredible price. Never again can I disdain someone because he is different. The barriers that separate us may be real and I may have genuine trouble hurdling them, but God has designed that we belong to one another. To the degree that I can overcome my reluctance and enter the doors to other people, whoever they are, to that degree will loneliness be diminished.

Then, he has given me a kingdom which is best expressed in "the one, holy, Christian and apostolic church." Not by blood or race or nation, but by faith, he draws us together into an eternal family. We who confess Jesus as Lord and Savior and who worship and follow him have a potential fellowship and oneness which nothing else on earth can rival.

We may have all sorts of differences—in wealth and station, in political loyalties, in esthetic tastes, in degrees of education, in the color of our skin—but these differences are but the diversities which give our oneness in Christ its rich character.

How sad it is that we so seldom, even in our own congregations, are caught up in the depth and height of this fellowship. It is there, and we know it is there, but we let its blessings slip through our hands. We assemble together on a Sunday morning, sit sedately and quietly in rows, pray and sing together, hear the glorious Word together, then with hardly a nod scatter to our separate and "lonely" places. We forget that for an hour we have been a microcosm of the magnificent company that is destined to live with God and with one another throughout eternity.

Loneliness has been called the trademark of our age. Vast forces, unleashed by the very blessings of technology, threaten to isolate us from one another or to draw us together for gain into artificial constellations. And despite, or perhaps because of, the growing population of the world, there is a tendency to dehumanize all relationships and to make each of us but a digit and a number. We are left with a vast vacuum of loneliness.

Against this, God has pitted himself with relentless warfare. He asks us to join him, and he opens many doors for us. Let us be vigilant to enter them.

Scripture: Ephesians 3:14-21

When I am lonely, O Lord, I am most likely without hope. I know you are nearer than the air I breathe, and that I can get your ear whenever I seek you. Help me to be an agent of yours to overcome loneliness in others. And let me understand and experience the blessings you have waiting for me in the great company of my fellow believers the world over and in my own congregation. Amen.

86

19

Some Simple
Disciplines

I don't have the answer to the world's great problems.
I have some answers for my own. They may be much
the same as yours, and you may have found the same
simple disciplines to cope with them.

The morning is the low point for me. I don't bounce
out of bed. I drift from a dream world into reality. If I
turn over for another moment of sleep, all the fears of
the world begin to attack. They swarm in like gnats, and
by the time I fumble around for my clothes, all hope for
the future is gone. I feel that the world is likely to fall
apart into utter chaos. Will it hold together another day?

By the time I've had some strong coffee, read some
prayers (by others of a more cheerful outlook) or psalms,
and have munched some breakfast, things look brighter.
I hardly dare introduce the day with the morning newspaper, except the comics and sports page. I'm really not
ready yet for the threatening headlines or the sober
editorials.

Getting to the office and becoming absorbed in the
routine of the day and hearing a few cheery good-morn-
ings from my friends, I have a mild reassurance that life
will go on and that the world's tenuous structures will
hold.

Now, as the morning wears on, I become reoriented

into the faith that has held me up across the years. God is still around, and God is God. That's really the nub of the matter, and that's the faith that keeps me going. I cannot know where precisely he is shaping the future or through whom he is making his decisive moves, but I know he is not vacationing on some distant star. He is in the thick of history.

I realize, of course, that he has given frightening freedoms to man and that man may thwart his will. I try not to be a romanticist and live in an Alice-in-Wonderland world. The selfishness and caprice of man has done and can do colossal damage and can cause untold suffering. I know this to be true, and even strong coffee can't dispel that fear.

I don't close my eyes altogether to the distant storm clouds that may gathering, but I turn to the tasks at hand. I would be derelict if I were to sit around brooding over a possible tornado and neglect the responsibilities of the moment.

I remember what Luther is supposed to have replied when someone asked him what he would do if the world were to end tomorrow. He said, "I would plant an apple tree." Or, what Ignatius Loyola, the founder of the Jesuit Order, said when he and two other student monks were playing a lawn game. One of them asked, "What would you do if the world were to come to an end in two hours?" The first student said he would go to church to pray. The other said he would go to be reconciled to his brother. Asked what he would do, Ignatius replied, "I would finish the game."

There is something basic and noble about being faithful to the everyday, commonplace tasks of life. Even a senator or a president, whose responsibilities fall in orbits of great power, cannot be the architects of history. They too, not knowing the ultimate outcome of their decisions or acts, must do what they must do from conscience and with integrity. They must not do less, they cannot do more.

While the mornings are a problem for me, I am not free of anxieties as I fall asleep at night. Then too fears over the future threaten to swarm in upon me. I begin to rehearse all the possible pitfalls that may beset me and my family. My night anxieties seem to zero in on *me*. The world-wide ones strike in the morning.

My best antidote to this night invasion is to begin making a mental list of all the blessings of the past, and to thank God for his long-range care of us. I don't have any trouble recalling an impressive index of his goodness. Then I remember a line from Cardinal Newman's great hymn, *Lead, Kindly Light:* "So long thy power has blessed me, sure it still will lead me on." By this time I probably have succeeded in depositing everything with God, and both peace and sleep engulf me.

I have discovered, too, that if I take on the problems and hurts of others (instead of my own) I have a sense of well-being. And is this not God's way? Has he not designed us to carry the cargo for another, and to let God carry my cargo? He has told us to bear one another's burdens, not simply as a duty but as a privilege of belonging to his kingdom.

In a dream a man found himself seated with others at a long table laden with food. But each man's arms were in splints at the elbow. Each could reach the food but was unable to bend his arm to bring the food to his mouth. Suddenly one man began feeding his neighbor across the table, and others followed, until the feast was in full swing, each doing for another.

But you say, all these disciplines or devices seem intent on finding tranquility and sleep. Is this not a cop-out? Did God create us for peace of mind and sleep?

Nietzsche in his *Thus Spake Zarathustra* has a satire on the kind of religion that seeks peace of mind. The essay is entitled, "How to Sleep Well." To sleep well, he says, you must work to become tired. Then you must play to become relaxed. Also, you must observe the virtues: do not steal, commit adultery, or murder. If you do, your conscience will keep you from sleep. One thing more is necessary, he says, to sleep well. You must put the virtues themselves to sleep at the proper time to sleep well. In other words, you must not take virtue too seriously. Otherwise, if you take on the high obligations of discipleship, you may be stark awake.

Of course God did not create us for sleep, or for peace of mind. He embroils us with his own purposes for this world. He gives us management, under him. He gives us all people as our brothers. He who bore a cross invites us to pick up a cross. He honors us with a chance to suffer with him.

But he also invites us to cast our cares on him. He assures us that we are not alone in our struggles for justice and mercy for all. He is at our side. To launch out alone is to fail and to be without hope. To rest back in him, and to be carried along by him into the thick of the world's hurts is to be at peace in the midst of the surging storms. He forgives us all our sins, he comforts us in all sorrows, he allays our fears—and he commissions us for his mission for the world.

As his children, we are entitled to peace. Jesus said, "My peace I give to you, not as the world gives." We do have a place of refuge. We offend him if we do not enter the door he opens for us. We find strange calm and strength as we enter.

90

Scripture: 1 Peter 4:12-19; 5:6-11

Help me, O Lord, to rest back into your care without escaping the duties you have for me. Let me find glory in the tasks near at hand. Reassure me from your many blessings of the past that my tomorrows too will be in your hands. My hope for all things rests finally in you. Amen.

20

Nothing But God

Man was made for God. This is the profoundest truth about him. Incidentally he was made to live on the earth, to have secondary needs like food and shelter. But his elemental need is God himself.

Just suppose that everything is gone. Health, friends, and job—all gone. Even the world itself—blown up. What is left? You and God are left. And in a profound sense, that is enough.

Two old people stood in the street watching their little home burn to the ground. This was all they had. Everything was gone. Mary took John's hand and said, "But, John, we have each other."

The shortest and most significant biography for any of us is simply, "He came from God and he returned to God, and in the meantime he lived with God." Everything else about us can be brushed aside and our lives still be fulfilled.

In his *Diary of an Old Soul*, George Macdonald has these lines,

> Not, Lord, that I have done well or ill,
> Not that my mind looks up to thee clear eyed,
> Not that it struggles in fast cerements tied,
> Not that I need thee daily, sorer still,
> Not that I, wretched, wander from thy will,

Not now for any cause to thee I cry, but this
That thou art thou, and here am I.

God and I together. This is enough. Nothing else really
matters. For I was created for him. With him I have all.

The psalmist in the 42nd Psalm cried out, "As a hart
longs for flowing streams, so longs my soul for thee, O
God. My soul thirsteth for God, for the living God." The
purest longing and yearning of the human being is not
for comfort or for love or even for the forgiveness of
sins, but for God himself. To live with him, whatever
that may add or subtract from anything else—simply
to live with him is the *summum bonum,* the greatest
good, for a human being.

Most of us fall far short of this purity of longing.
We tend to want to use God. We are not altogether
comfortable with having him around. We want him, to
be sure, but we want him as a resource for the other
things we may want, like we want a rich uncle who can
help us out. But to have the uncle in our homes, month
after month, may be another matter.

We want security, and God may give us that. We want
the promise of things for the future, like peace and
prosperity. We want peace of mind, the wiping out of
our sins and guilt. We want fulfillment. Who but God
can deliver this kind of an order? So, we cry for God.

But God is God. He is not our servant. He is not
someone who deposits a hundred thousand dollars in
the bank to our account, and then stays away. He is
not a means toward an end. He is the end! Everything
he does is designed to have us rejoin him. Nothing
else, really.

Whenever we list the rich gifts of God, we risk rele-
gating God to the giver of gifts and not to the possessor
of our souls. And he does give rich gifts. He gives us

the forgiveness of our sins. He gives us the joy of his creation. He gives us management of this earth. He gives us title to the limitless wealth of his kingdom. He gives us heaven itself.

But all this is finally incidental. He gives us himself!

When we say, "Hope in the Lord," what really are we saying? Are we telling one another that the way to have a future without war, without hunger, without injustice, without meaninglessness is to employ God? Are we enlisting him as an ally who can help us with our plans and our aspirations and our hopes? Or are we turning everything over to him, satisfied that whatever he designs for us is good, as long as we have him, and he has us?

The tragedy of the Garden of Eden was not that Adam and Eve lost the garden but that they lost God. They ran away from him. They separated themselves from him. And God's great plan of redemption in Christ Jesus had one supreme purpose—to return man to God. The cross, with the removal of man's sin and guilt, was God's way of removing the barrier that separated man from him, in order that man might again live with him. The forgiveness of sins is not some sort of psychological gimmick which will guarantee peace of mind. It is God's gigantic maneuver in time to restore man to himself.

Being returned to God, we are of course freed from the burden of guilt and sin. Through the work of Christ for us, we need carry no cargo of the past into the presence of God. But being with God, we may indeed find ourselves embracing a new kind of cargo—the burdens of God himself for this bewildered and blundering world.

I must confess that when I set out to thank God I gravitate to a list of all the blessings he gives me. I make an inventory. I enumerate things like health, a free country, a loving family, friends, work to do, eyes to see color, ears to hear music. I rarely say simply, "God, I thank you for you."

But is this not the supreme gift, after all? And whatever else I hope for and claim as his gifts to me, ought I not always return to the overwhelming fact that, come what may for me and for my world, my deepest hopes are realized in the assurance that I have been returned to him?

And should I not rather thank him that he honors me with tasks to do for him? He is active in the world of sin. He understands the hurts of people and of nations better than any of us. He is as deeply involved as a cross. In every struggle against injustice, loneliness, pride, envy, greed, indifference—he is in the thick of the fray, pitting himself against the forces that destroy his children. And having come back to him, I thank and honor him most by joining him in this glorious involvement.

Until the end, however, I keep thanking him for himself. I may find little satisfaction in the outcome of the struggles. The world may wheel on to its destruction. The forces of evil are strong. But come what may, losing one battle after another, I need never lose him. Nothing in all creation can separate me from his love.

Of course he gives rich gifts and rewards. We need place no limits on what he has in store for his children on earth. The next century could yield unpredictable good on this earth for the next generations. And heaven itself promises fulfillment of indescribable wonder for us. But it would be a pity if a lover were to find his beloved appealing because she cooked him such exotic meals, and it would be tragic if we found God attractive because he delivered such wonderful gifts.

Quite apart from any gifts, God himself is the great gift. Having him we have all.

Scripture: Psalm 42

Dear God, I confess that I am so captured by the presence and the promise of all your gifts to me that I become beguiled by them and forget that you, yourself, are the great gift. Help me to want you, gifts or no gifts, and help me to thank you for you. Amen.